Par

Parent Talk

Celebrities take a sideways
look at being a parent

Compiled by
Steve Chalke

Hodder & Stoughton

British Library Cataloguing in Publication Data
A record for this book is available from the British Library

ISBN 0 340 78516 0

Printed and bound in Great Britain by
Clays Ltd, St Ives PLC

Hodder & Stoughton
A Division of Hodder Headline Ltd
338 Euston Road
London NW1 3BH

Introduction

A very elderly, but happy-looking, 90-year-old lady wandered into her local village post office.

'You look pleased with yourself', the assistant commented.

'I am', she beamed, *'Today I finally got my youngest son, aged 70, into an old people's home!'*

Being a parent is a job for life. In fact, as a father of four, it's my considered opinion that it's without doubt the most ongoingly demanding and challenging task that any of us ever undertakes. But though one moment it tests you to breaking point, the next it brings untold joy and seems like the most exciting job in the universe.

I sometimes think the best way of describing parenthood is to compare it to riding a never-ending roller coaster. Countless highs and lows; endless joys and struggles.

Ernest Hemingway wrote a story about a Spanish father and son who have a serious argument and fall out with one another. As a result the son leaves home and runs away to Madrid.

Many years pass until, finally, the lonely father

decides to attempt a reconciliation. He travels to Madrid where he believes that his son still lives and takes out a small ad in the city's *El Liberal* newspaper. It simply reads:

'Paco meet me at the Hotel Montana noon Tuesday. All is forgiven. Papa.'

The father has no idea whether his son will even read the paper, let alone want to see him again. Imagine his surprise, then, when he arrives in the square at the appointed time to find himself faced with 800 young men – all named Paco and all longing for reunion with their estranged fathers.

We all make mistakes as parents – there is no such thing as the perfect mum or dad. But here is a great truth. Your child needs you. They need you desperately. This means that, whatever your family situation, your child has an in-built desire to forgive your mistakes and overlook your shortcomings. Put bluntly, they love you and their relationship with you is one of the most important in their life.

So here they are, the collected thoughts of parents and children from all walks of public life – lessons learnt, eccentric families, pieces of advice, funny anecdotes – they're all here as a celebration of parenthood. And as I've collected them, one thought has struck me more profoundly than any other – there is no such thing as the perfect family. We are all in the same boat. We love the ideal, but struggle with the reality of parenthood and family life ... whoever we are.

So enjoy! And whatever else you do – keep going!

Steve Chalke
London 2000

Thank you to all those who responded to my constant pestering and, in spite of frantic diaries, gave me an insight into their lives either as parents or children.

Thanks also to Charles and Judith at Hodder and Stoughton for letting me do it, Maggie Doherty at Parentalk for keeping me at it and, most of all, James Griffin who worked ceaselessly to make it happen.

Kids never fail to amuse or surprise me. Although I think I'm a fairly laid back kinda Dad, I've still always been quite strict with them about manners. It really bugs me when kids don't say 'please' or 'thank you' so I've been boringly tough on mine about always asking for something nicely and being grateful for things they receive.

When Toby was about five, he was having real trouble remembering to say his please and thank yous (sometimes he still does!). One day, after asking me if he could have some sweets while we were in the paper shop, he looked very despondent when I said to him 'No, Toby. You're not getting any sweets until you say the magic word ... now try again!'

'OK, Daddy,' he replied. 'Can I have some sweets abracadabra!'

(CHRIS TARRANT)

Radio DJ and TV presenter

There is no training for being a parent. People least qualified to be parents often are parents. We are all frail and inadequate. But all that is required is that you love your children (and show them that you do) and in time, when they leave home, they will love you in return. Be kind to children because kindness is 'love in action'!

(WILLIAM ROACHE)
Ken Barlow in *Coronation Street*

When I asked a friend what the worst years of raising children are, he replied with the wisdom of a father of seven: 'the first thirty years!'

This wry observation is only rivalled by the thought that no one ever says on their death bed, 'I wish I'd spent more time at the office.' We should cherish the

I KNOW NOBODY REGRETS BEING A GOOD PARENT ON THEIR DEATH BED - BUT I WISH THIS BED WAS A LOT LESS LIVELY RIGHT NOW.

BOUNCE!

opportunities to share in our children's lives, their fears and their dreams.

David Alton.
(DAVID ALTON)
Professor
the Lord Alton of Liverpool

When our eldest, Ben, was learning to talk we were sitting in the kitchen and, with a sense of purpose, he turned to his mother and said 'Mummy, I really love you!'

Tears welled up in our eyes, our lips trembled and we felt we were about to have a real bonding moment – the sort we'd remember forever. Then Ben turned around, looked at the cooker and said, 'Aga, I love you too!'

Oh well. Next time maybe ...

(SIMON MAYO)
BBC Radio One DJ

At a rather formal occasion, our son, aged three at the time, let out a very loud fart. Hastily reminding him of his manners, I asked him, 'What do you say?'

He replied in a questioning voice, 'Thank you for having me?'

(JEREMY CLARKSON)
Journalist

My parents were very young when they had me, which was great because they were always interested in my street-cred and reputation!

The main trait I inherited from their youthfulness was independence. So much so that one morning, aged two, I woke up around 4 a.m. and left the house in my nightie with my pram and doll! I walked around for ages – quite happily, although wondering why it was so quiet! My neighbour eventually found me and delivered me home to my parents. When they saw me, rather than giving me a good telling off and injecting me with their own anxiety, they just hugged me – delighted at my safe return!

Their confidence gave me a great sense of adventure and I know that I'll endeavour to care for my children without wrapping them in cotton wool.

Tamzin Outhwaite

(TAMZIN OUTHWAITE)

Melanie Healy in *EastEnders*

I am always saying to the children, 'I love you very much <u>but</u> ... please don't interrupt me ... turn the telly down ... be quiet ... clear this mess up ...' etc.

Then the other day I was trying to talk to my daughter when she turned to me and said, 'I love you very much, Mummy, but I'm trying to watch <u>Bob the Builder</u>!'

(FERN BRITTON)
TV presenter

I don't want to give the impression I was inexperienced with children, but I still can't believe that when I first picked up my baby daughter her head didn't fall off!

(PETER KRYSOWSKI)

Film producer

My Mum still tells me to always wear a vest! I have to confess I don't always. But other advice has been really useful ... Thanks, Mum!

(PHILIPPA FORRESTER)

Presenter *Tomorrow's World*

One night when I was about eight years old I said to my mum as I was climbing into bed, 'Do you believe that the tooth fairy is real, Mam?'

She replied by asking me if I thought she was.

'Yes!' I replied enthusiastically.

'Then if you believe she is real, then she is!' she said.

I've always found this extremely useful. It helped me realise that I didn't have to think like everyone else, and that having different beliefs and opinions to the majority can be a good thing. I learnt to respect other people's points of view and not to be afraid of my own.

(JILL HALFPENNY)
Rebecca Hopkins in *Coronation Street*

When we came to Britain from India, my father had to spend his entire wealth on our fares. As a result he arrived in the UK with just £5 in his pocket, and the daunting task of having a wife and four children to house, feed and clothe. But he was a man of prayer who never complained and never stopped trusting God.

So from my dad I learned to trust God and pray. Through his example I knew what real faith was. I learnt to depend on God in the tough times as well as the good ones – to keep praying and not let go. I learnt that you can't just be a believer when it's all going your way and that real strength of character comes through the way you handle the bad times.

(SIR CLIFF RICHARD)
Performer

I was on TV recently, talking about infertility and my personal experience of IVF, which was finally successful with twins after three attempts.

The programme producer wanted to feature my children so I decided they would have to be told about IVF. I certainly didn't want them finding out from other children at school.

I explained that Mummy and Daddy wanted children so very badly but that, unfortunately, there was something wrong with Mummy's tummy so we had to go to the doctor who told us we could have children using IVF. This meant the doctors taking two of Mummy's eggs and Daddy's sperm, putting them together in a glass dish until they joined and then putting them back into Mummy's tummy where they grew into Kyla and Natalie.

Amazingly, the children seemed to take all this in except the word 'sperm'. They explained the whole story back to me, just sticking on that word.

'I know,' said Natalie. 'Let's make a song about sperm and then we'll remember it.'

What could I say? They both proceeded to sing to the tune of 'London Bridge is Falling Down':

Sperm, sperm, sperm, sperm,
   sperm, sperm, sperm,
Sperm, sperm, sperm, sperm,
   sperm, sperm,
Sperm, sperm, sperm, sperm,
   sperm, sperm, sperm,
Sperm, sperm, sperm, sperm.

I just hope they didn't teach anyone that song at school!

Cheryl Baker

(CHERYL BAKER)

TV presenter

Though I was brought up in Britain, my upbringing was heavily influenced by my Sri Lankan heritage. My father used to remind me of a Tamil proverb: 'A man waits for the day when he walks into a room and is introduced, not in his own right, but simply as his son's father.'

In other words, a parent has done their job well when it's the child's name and achievements that are foremost in people's minds. As parents it is our duty to nurture our children, to offer

WE'RE GLAD YOU RESPECT THE WISDOM OF THE ELDERLY...

...BUT YOU'RE STILL DOING YOUR HOMEWORK BY YOURSELF!

them opportunities that we never had and, ultimately, to empower them to move away from our shadow.

But Tamil culture also places, in return, an obligation on the child. There comes a moment in a child's life when he must take the lead, when he must take responsibility for his parents' welfare.

Respect for the wisdom of the elderly, due deference to age – these are core values in Asian society. They have, though, a relevance for all peoples regardless of race or status.

(GEORGE ALAGIAH)

Journalist and Presenter, BBC News

One moment left me eternally grateful to my dad and taught me a lot about what helps when you've got a problem. It was 1964, I was a 19-year-old student and pregnant. My dad was a committed, locally high-profile headmaster and an unmarried pregnant teenager could have spelled public shame.

But when I, white as a sheet and sick with anxiety, broke the news, he didn't utter one word of reproach or anger. He knew I knew I'd messed up. He was sad for me but, if anything, blamed himself for not making sure I was better informed. He didn't make a drama out of it but listened quietly while I told my story and helped me find out what choices I had.

In spite of other ups and downs we had over the years, that moment showed me how much he truly loved me. If my kids run into crises, I remember how special

that felt and try to give them that same
uncritical, unconditional support when
they're down.

(DEIDRE SANDERS)

Agony aunt for the *Sun*

I was leading the Tournament at the Benson and Hedges International Open by one shot before the last day. This was a tournament I'd always wanted to win, having thrown it away a couple of times, and so I was feeling decidedly nervous.

On the final day, I took my family with me to the course, to leave the children in the crèche while Eimear walked around with me. The idea was that if I played well, they could all come down at the last green to share the moment (or cheer me up if I didn't play so well!)

Tish, my very sociable 3-year-old daughter, managed to get hold of all my nerves and anticipation and put this whole thing in perspective for me by saying as we drove up to the clubhouse, 'Daddy, why is there a golf course at this crèche?'

I'm pleased to say I won!

(signature)

(COLIN MONTGOMERIE)

Golfer

How unpredictable are our genes. My mother has beautiful skin, elegant arms and legs, needs very little sleep and has no notion of what it means to have a sweet tooth. And what do I inherit from her ... Bunions!!!"

(DIANE LOUISE JORDAN)
Presenter

Parenting is surely one of the great paradoxes of life. Place a job advert in the local newspaper – 'Sleepless nights (whether the kids are in or out!), financial black-hole, taxi driver, compulsory attendance of mediocre amateur dramatic occasions, etc.' – and you would hardly expect to be trampled in the crush of applicants. Yet millions of us take the plunge and, for the most part, we never regret it in the least.

WHAT DOES TRIPLE JUMPING HAVE IN COMMON WITH PARENTING?

NEITHER OF THEM WORK IF YOU BURY YOUR HEAD IN THE SAND...

Certainly this is certainly my experience. Although I still feel far too young to be collecting two boys from school each day, my wife Alison, Sam and Nathan are the joy of my life. Family life is nothing if not relentless, but it has enriched all of our lives, individually and together, more than we could ever articulate.

Now where did that application form get to ...?

(JONATHAN EDWARDS)
Triple Jumper

Let me say first that I never believe in lying ... unless it's Monday morning, you're rushing your 5-year-old through the tube barrier and you're too late for school to stop for a child's ticket.

ISN'T THAT THE CARTOONIST BLOKE?

YES-BUT HIS REPUTATION IS GONE DOWN THE TUBES.

EXCESS FARES →

'How old is that child?' asks the ticket collector

'Er ... four' I stammer (making a mental note to give a tenner to charity if I can get away with this, just this once).

I'll never know if I <u>would</u> have because, at this point, my son Pearse chimes in with 'I'm not four Dad, I'm <u>FIVE</u>. We had my birthday last week. Don't you remember?'

Needless to say you could have heard him five stations away ... and these days we always get up in time to buy a ticket!

John Byrne

(JOHN BYRNE)

Cartoonist and comedy writer

I always respected my father and mother and was extremely grateful for everything they did for me in their lifetime.

Dickie Bird

(DICKIE BIRD)

Retired cricket umpire

When my daughter Laura was ten, I decided she was old enough for a chat about the Internet. I used very simple language and was careful not to speak too fast. I am delighted to say that after only half an hour I understood it! Now that she is twelve, she has promised to teach me about e-commerce.

JOHN TAYLOR
The Lord Taylor of Warwick

I have a vivid memory of being a parent to teenagers. I arrived home, forty-eight hours late, exhausted and anxious, after a nearly lethal journey back from a conference in Greece. I knew my family would be frantic with worry about what had happened to me. I came in into the welcoming sanctity of my home to find my 13-year-old daughter on her own in the sitting-room.

'Alice', I cried with relief, 'I'm home, safe at last!'

'Shhh', she hissed. 'Can't you see I'm watching TV!'

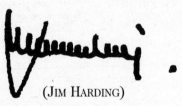

(JIM HARDING)
Former Chief Executive, NSPCC

We left the house hurriedly in order to beat the traffic to our holiday destination in the north of England. No sooner were we out of London when my son Aston started demanding his beloved blanket: a canary-yellow cot cover which had to follow him around everywhere, completely inseparable! In a crazed panic I frantically turned the car upside down to no avail. My husband had obviously forgotten to pack it!

There was nothing left for me to do. I whipped off my petticoat and put it into Aston's clenched hands. His body relaxed, as did his relieved parents. As soon as we returned from our holiday I bought him an identical blanket so that I would never have to compromise my modesty in the name of harmony again.

(FLOELLA BENJAMIN)

TV presenter

We did what most excited parents do when their new baby is on the way. The nursery was decorated, the Moses basket was given a new mattress (we had two children already), the nappies were sorted and the sleep-suits and vests were arranged neatly in the drawers.

I then learned a lesson that has helped prepare me for the uncertainty that being a parent brings – I woke up from a caesarean section to discover I had twins!

Out went the Moses basket – too small – they slept together. Baby-grows were put in the cupboard – the twins were so tiny they needed dolls' clothes; the single buggy, now useless, became a garden toy and shares in Pampers suddenly rose!

We're sometimes tempted to believe that our children will do and behave as we would choose. The reality is that children and teenagers are unpredictable and being a parent is full of surprises!

(signature)

(RUTH HARDING)

Patron of Refuge

My mum and dad loved to sing. Dad in the car on long journeys and Mum while she polished and dusted! My brother and I were fortunate to have lived in a house full of happy song.

One of my favourite memories is hair-washing night. Mum used to dry my curls in front of the fire while I sat on her knee. She would lustily sing my favourite songs, like

GREAT NEWS, MUM! WE THOUGHT WE'D HELP YOU PRACTISE 'SMOKE GETS IN YOUR EYES..

...SO WE SET FIRE TO THE CURTAINS.

'The little boy that Santa forgot', as she carefully dried my hair.

I know the words of many of the old standards and I'm sure watching my mum's passionate renditions of 'Smoke gets in your eyes' and 'Old man river' fed my longings to go on the stage.

Mum confessed to me when we were both older that she had always wanted to be a singer but instead she gave her love and care to the family – singing joyfully all the while. I'll always be grateful.

Wendy Craig

(WENDY CRAIG)

Actress

Playing in the band often means being away on tour and especially travelling throughout the USA. Every time I leave I sit with my daughter Ellie and tell her that Dad is going to America to do some singing.

Several weeks after returning from one such trip, I had to nip up to the shop to get some milk, only to find on my return a little girl on the doorstep saying, 'Daddy, have you just been to America!'

(MARTIN SMITH)
Singer/songwriter

AND THE FORECAST FOR PARENTS: OCCASIONAL STORMCLOUDS BUT LOTS OF SILVER LININGS.

The thing I most appreciate about being a parent is picking up dirty cups and clothes and not knowing where any of my borrowed possessions have got to!

Michael Fish

(MICHAEL FISH)
BBC weatherman

I remember when I was about ten and a half we went on a family day out. The usual sort of stuff – endless rounds of so-called beautiful buildings and gushing fountains! However, one particular fountain did capture my imagination, and I began to dream and make wishes as I threw in three pennies. I really wished hard for a pony, ideally the one owned by our neighbour, named Tiddleywinks, which I'd ridden before.

My birthday morning arrived a few months later and my father told me that before I was to open my presents I was to check on our two heifers at the end of the garden. I rushed off to perform my task, but as I walked down the garden noticed three large backsides facing me, one of which was clearly not a cow! My pony, saddled and ready to go – Tiddleywinks!

My parents were waiting at the back door as I flew back to them. As a parent myself I can only imagine their delight in my joy. I only hope that, as I have grown into adulthood, I have managed to give a little to my beloved parents, without whom I would have achieved nothing.

Lynda Bellingham.

(LYNDA BELLINGHAM)
Actress and former 'Oxo Mum'

Several years ago I was invited to start the London Marathon which begins in Greenwich Park near to our home in Blackheath. As I was walking to the starting point I spotted a family sitting on the grass and stopped to speak with them. There were two children, Jamie aged six and Janice aged four. After a brief chat I went on my way, started the Marathon, returned home and forgot all about the conversation.

A week later I received a letter from the lady to whom I had spoken. 'Mr Waite,' she said, 'the other morning I was sitting with my children waiting for the Marathon to start, when I saw you coming across the heath. I said to them, 'Oh, look! There's Terry Waite, he was a hostage for five years'.

To our surprise you came across and spoke with us. Did you notice little Janice staring at you? When you went away she said, 'Mummy, is it true? Was that man really an ostrich for five years?'

Terry Waite.

(TERRY WAITE CBE)

Former Special Envoy for the Archbishop
of Canterbury and Beirut hostage

My 4-year-old son was listening to a conversation I was having with my husband. I was discussing a close friend's relationship as I was not impressed with her choice of partner.

Then one day, when she came round, my son burst into the room and shouted, 'My mom said that your boyfriend is using you and you can't even see it. You're too good for him!'

I looked at her and immediately said, 'He watches too much <u>Oprah</u>!'

(ANGIE LE MAR)
Comedienne/actress/writer

Here's some advice for teenagers ... Listen to your parents, they know what they're talking about (most of the time)!

Sometimes you may not agree with the decisions they make but try to look beyond them – there's usually a logical reason why they made them.

Always appreciate your parents – because they won't be there forever.

Carly Hillman

(CARLY HILLMAN)

Nicky di Marco in *EastEnders*

49

We have three young sons, all under four years old! Before they came along, I never realised the full importance of my mother's advice that what children want is a parent's time – above all else.

My father had a very busy job which took him away most evenings, so my sister and I spent very little quality time with him. I have been determined to avoid a repeat. I resist any weekend work commitments (when I can), and always rush home after work to catch bath-time and put the boys to bed.

Bonding is not one of those meaningless concepts – it is the rewarding product of time spent with the boys. Children know from a young age when you're avoiding them (even subconsciously) and it's essential to include them in all kinds of activities – even when they slow you down! There's no

better investment in a child's upbringing.
Give your time generously as a parent,
and you will be well rewarded.

Huw Edwards

(HUW EDWARDS)

Journalist and Presenter, BBC News

When I was in my twenties, I lived at home, but frequently spent the night at friends' houses. To this end I carried a 6ft piece of foam mattress in the back seat of my car.

My mother, however, couldn't work out what the foam sheet was for. Eventually she tentatively enquired, 'Is it some kind of contraceptive device, dear?'

It seems sex education, even among the married, was a lot more primitive then!

Carol Barnes

(CAROL BARNES)
Presenter, ITN News

An angry 11-year-old boy skated over to his free-skate coach and declared, 'This is stupid!' after falling repeatedly on his practice jumps.

'Well, don't do it, then,' his coach replied. The boy gave up his free skating.

A few days later the same angry 11-year-old pulled away from his ice-dance partner at 6.30 a.m. and skated over to his ice-dance coach. 'This is stupid!' he declared.

'Go and do it again,' his coach replied.

The boy went on to represent his country in the Olympics at ice dancing.

The free-skating coach was his father, the ice-dance coach his mother.

Oh yes, for the men reading this – the father invested in the boy's schooling. He didn't give up ... just took another tack!

Nicky

(NICKY SLATER)
Ice skater

I made my television debut with a very tiny part in a production of <u>Peer Gynt</u>. My mother ordered all of the neighbours to watch and they duly did.

When one of them observed that I hadn't been in it much, my mother hit back with, 'That's because you've only got a small screen, we've got a 24-inch – he was on all the time on ours!'

David Neilson

(DAVID NEILSON)

Roy Cropper in *Coronation Street*

One thing I'll always thank my dad for is helping me escape the torment of being dragged round the shops on a Saturday morning in Norwich by my mum and my two sisters. When I was a lot younger, a Saturday trip to Norwich for a weekly shop was as much a part of our calendar as Christmas. My dad knew how much I detested spending hours in Laura Ashley and M&S, and so would take me to our favourite fish stall in the city's market, where we'd enjoy a saucer of fresh prawns and a chin-wag. A simple thing, but over the years I've come to realise that this was a small, but important part of my relationship with my Dad.

We still go back when I'm home; but now I buy the prawns, and they're frozen instead of fresh!

(SIMON THOMAS)

Blue Peter Presenter

My sister Linda is four years younger than me, and although she seems shy and reserved, she is actually far more determined than I'll ever be. One day when I was nine we were drawing at the dining table. Mum was in the next room reading on a rocking chair.

Linda pushed a piece of paper in front of me and said, 'Look what I've done – it's a horse.'

I replied in true older-sister fashion, 'Well, it's not very good – it's only got three legs!'

Linda snatched up her drawing and showed Mum, telling her what I'd said. Looking up from her book Mum said, 'It doesn't matter, Linda, it's a very good horse' and carried on reading. For a moment there was silence, as Mum and I continued to read and draw. And then – whoosh! Back went the rocking chair and Mum fell flat.

'IT DOES MATTER!' screamed my 5-year-old sister, purple in the face. And with that she ran and locked herself in the bathroom. It took hours to talk her out!

Linda is twenty-seven now and if ever we're trying to sort anything out in our family, the words you'll always hear are 'It <u>does</u> matter!'

Andrea X

(ANDREA MCLEAN)

GMTV presenter

Being a parent can be quite a trial,
You can feel your gorge rising
With poisonous bile.
One day you are sane
The next quite mad
For one thing we're not taught
Is to be Mum and Dad.

It comes like a thunderbolt
Comes like a shot
Comes as a wondrous jolt
Ready or not.
Are you up for the journey?
Are you up for the job?
Should they wheel in the gurney
As you slobber and slob?

And then! When you bend
Down over the crib
And see the result
Of the thing that you did
With that pink little face

And that dear rosebud mouth
So sweet at the north
Not so at the south ...

Your heart swells with love
Like it's going to explode
And you know there and then
You can shoulder the load.
The road will be long
But now you belong
To a club built on love
And that makes you strong.

Richard O'Brien

(RICHARD O'BRIEN)
TV presenter

I can honestly say that, although it's hard work, parenting is the most rewarding experience I've ever had. One morning I explained to Elliott, my 6-year-old, that Mummy was very tired and asked him to leave me to doze while he grabbed some breakfast.

After a while I heard him creep into my bedroom with his little sister in tow. He turned to her and said, 'Shhh ... Mummy's sleeping – doesn't she look just like an angel when she's asleep?'

I'd often wondered if he was always asleep when I went in to check on him. Now I know he wasn't!

Sharon Davies

(SHARON DAVIES)

Former Olympic swimmer and TV presenter

We were new to the area and had been invited to afternoon tea by a delightful elderly couple, old and valued friends of our own parents. We coached the children, aged four and six, carefully – to tell them their names, to give our hosts the flowers they had picked, to eat their tea nicely and quietly, as old people didn't like a lot of noise; then they could go and play in the garden.

They carried out our instructions exactly. We stood on the doorstep and when our hostess opened the door our youngest gave her the flowers and said 'Hello – My name's Esther – Here are your flowers – Where's the old man?'

(DR JOHN TRIPP)

Senior lecturer in child health, Exeter University

I was recently playing Twenty Questions with my 7-year-old daughter who had a famous person lodged in her mind. By the last question I had ascertained it was a famous female from history, but it wasn't Elizabeth I, Helen of Troy, or Cleopatra. So I gave up.

'It's Julia Caesar,' she said triumphantly. From that moment on, I vowed to do more work with her at home!

Jane Moore

(JANE MOORE)

Columnist in the *Sun* and TV presenter

My son is fascinated by <u>Thomas the Tank Engine</u>, especially when the trains crash. I don't think his enthusiasm was shared by the people around us, though, on a recent flight to Dublin.

We hit some turbulence and my son announced loudly, 'Plane crashing, Mummy!'

Fiona Farrell.

(FIONA FARRELL)

TV presenter

Think of the influence we have on our children, or the influence our parents had on us. Is there anything that made more of a difference – not just for a moment, but for a lifetime? Which one of us doesn't carry some memory of words our parents said to us when we were young – words that hurt, or words that make us walk tall?

Those are the words we never forget, and they shape our image of who we are. If they hurt, we can spend much of our adult life

trying to ease the pain. But if they gave us pride or confidence, it is that which will stay with us through the years. Tell your child you love her, you love him, and in that one act of letting them know they are loved, you give them the strength to love in return. I don't know of a greater gift; and all it takes is a few seconds of our time, and our heart.

Jonathan Sacks

(PROFESSOR JONATHAN SACKS)
The Chief Rabbi

No teenage birthday these days seems complete without a sleep-over. One weekend we had a house full of teenage girls and, late on the Saturday morning, I was in the kitchen cooking a full English breakfast for a dozen young people.

While I was frying the eggs I sensed my daughter at my arm watching closely how I was doing it. In a flash, I saw myself as a child watching my own father doing the same thing, and realised how I was doing it in

HAVE YOUR PARENTS TAUGHT YOU TO COOK BREAKFAST YET?

WELL I'M NOT OLD ENOUGH TO FRY EGGS BUT I'VE MASTERED THE BIT WHERE DAD SAYS "GROOGH! I'VE GOT A TERRIBLE HANGOVER!"

exactly the same way. I wondered if, in a few years time she would be cooking eggs for her children in the same way their great-grandfather did.

What you do and what you are engrave a bigger impression on your children's character that what you actually tell them. There's a built-in tendency to mimic those around you (just think of how your accent can change depending on who you're talking to) and this imitation is especially true in the formative years of childhood.

Which of our characteristics do we want our children to imitate?

(THE RT REVD JAMES JONES)
Bishop of Liverpool

My mum – always the first to cry at a sloppy film ('Stop it Ju, you've set me off ...) and the first to sneer at all things superstitious. She still scrubs the front step every Saturday and boasts the cleanest kitchen in Lancashire! But most of all she's always on my side.

My dad – Saturday afternoons, cricket matches, whistled hymns, noodle-doodles on toast and our secret gobbledegook language that still drives Mum mad. He sometimes thinks his soft heart is his downfall – but it's not his downfall, it's his saving grace.

Julie Hesmondhalgh

(JULIE HESMONDHALGH)

Hayley Cropper in *Coronation Street*

*B*eing the mom of twin girls (now nineteen years old!) has taught me so many lessons. Easily the biggest though, and therefore the best advice I could offer to any mum or dad in a similar situation, is to let each of your kids develop their own personality.

So often twins are expected to go around together, do everything together, even dress the same. Although they shared a lot of interests, Alicia and Alexandria were also encouraged to do their own thing – different school classes, different ballet lessons, different groups of friends and so on.

I think they've been all the better for it, so give your twins a bit of room to claim their own turf – and they'll thank you for it!

Sheila D. Ferguson

(SHEILA FERGUSON)

Singer, actress and performer

I was nineteen and in love! My boyfriend had just proposed and I was ecstatic! It was 1965 and we earned very little money. I spent many lunch hours gazing in shop windows at the displays of sparkling gems, all the time knowing that the only ring we could afford would be small. Eventually I spotted one I loved the look of in an antique shop window. My heart sank, however, when I heard it cost £45 – our budget was £35 maximum and we simply couldn't afford the extra £10.

I explained the situation to my mother. Always resourceful, she suggested that we'd go to the shop together to haggle, but also take a couple of her antique plates with us to barter with! The shopkeeper was so impressed with the lengths we went to he eventually said, 'OK, well, if you're that desperate to have the ring you had better have it!'

That ring was my pride and joy for thirty

years, and when my daughter became engaged, I gave it to her fiancé to give to her. It is a very special ring, and is still as beautiful today.

(ROSEMARY CONLEY)
Fitness guru

Gazing lovingly at your newborn daughter is one thing, but it's quite another to open her school lunchbox nine years down the line and discover a frog sitting happily among the crusts and satsuma peel – believe me!

Janice

(JANICE FIXTER)

Author of *The Parentalk Guide to Being a Mum*

My three children all play the violin and they each began playing at the age of three, following the Suzuki method where they play together with groups of other children. My daughter Scarlett's debut was at the Queen Elizabeth Hall, London, in front of several thousand people at the tender age of five. She proudly stood in the front row but unfortunately for Scarlett as she lifted her violin to her chin she unknowingly took her dress and petticoat with it – they had got caught in the violin! Her M&S knickers were on view to the entire audience who burst into laughter. Scarlett, however, following instructions to look only at the leader and concentrate on the music, continued to play totally unaware that she was the cause of such merriment.

Annabel Karmel.

(ANNABEL KARMEL)

Children's cookery author

As one of four children (two boys and two girls), there was always a good deal of physical friction, especially between the boys and girls. Once, upon being reprimanded by my father for fighting with my sister, I mitigated that she had started it by hitting me.

My father replied, 'That's different – she's a girl!'

(SIMON BIAGI)
TV presenter

My mother gave me one piece of advice. Very short but very lasting. She said, 'You can achieve anything you really want to achieve.'

(JOAN ARMATRADING)

Singer and songwriter

On a journey to a local restaurant, my middle son (then aged four) was becoming bored so I struck up a conversation with him about what he was going to eat when we arrived.

'I'll have nuggets, chips and 'mato ketchup,' he cried with a rekindled sense of excitement.

'Sounds great,' I replied. 'But it's not 'mato ketchup, it's tomato ketchup. Try and say it again – to-to-to-mato ketchup.'

'No, Mum, I only want one 'mato ketchup and chips and nuggets!!'

Sheryl Gascoigne

(SHERYL GASCOIGNE)
Former wife of Paul Gascoigne

My eldest daughter spent her first two months in a special care unit because she was born prematurely.

One day I was talking to her consultant when he gave me some advice. 'Never forget,' he said, 'that when it comes to your child, you're the expert.'

Whenever I've dealt with any professional since about any of my children, I've always kept that in mind. They may be an expert in paediatrics, education, dentistry, nursing, dancing, swimming, or Brownies, but I'm the one who's the expert on my daughter.

Joanna

(JOANNA MOORHEAD)
Journalist and author

In Uganda we have a proverb which says, 'It takes a whole village to raise a child.' This is how I grew up in Uganda; not only with my parents' love, but with the involvement of everyone who lived around me. Our identity is not a separate individualism but, as we say: 'I am, because we are.'

My own children were raised not in a village but in south London where I was vicar for many years. But the proverb still applied. The family of the church and the local community was our village where they received

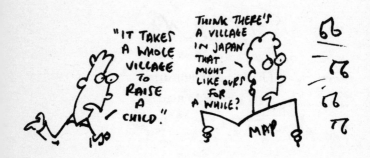

78

love and care, discipline and wisdom from all its members. And not only the children because I too continued to be 'raised' by their encouragement and support as well as the occasional loving rebuke!

(THE RT REVD DR JOHN SENTAMU)
Bishop of Stepney

I am blessed with two beautiful, talented and academically brilliant daughters. But puberty and early adulthood are funny things. Both went off to a distant planet. Only one returned. The other will always be welcomed – even with grandchildren! Especially ...

Ian McCaskill

(IAN McCASKILL)

BBC weatherman

Being a non-parent can make you the most popular person in the world. You can 'borrow' children for the day, let them run wild, spoil them rotten – knowing they are going to be picked up and taken away! Best of all, you know that when they're told off at home they will always say:

'Why can't I? Auntie Maggie always lets me ...!'

Maggie

(MAGGIE KOUMI)

Editor, *Hello* magazine

I'd always wondered how my parents had failed ever to get into rock music – they apparently didn't even notice the Beatles – so one day I told my dad I'd take him to a concert.

We went to see Elvis Costello at the Royal Albert Hall and sat up in the circle, all very civilised. After a couple of songs, a solitary man in the stalls tried to wander forwards, presumably to get a better view. 'Uh-oh,' said my dad. 'Trouble!'

I think he thought he was seeing the beginning of a riot! The man was politely turned back by a bouncer and returned to his seat!

Jeremy

(JEREMY VINE)
Presenter, BBC *Newsnight*

Going from no children to three step-children was a bit of a shock! My initiation took place one Sunday lunchtime when Claudia (then three years old), left the table to go to the bathroom. Five minutes later she was calling my name.

The rest of the family all giggled and said she wanted me to go and wipe her bottom! At this point in my life I had only ever wiped my own! The look on my face made the others descend into heaps of laughter!

Her next comment to me one morning, whilst discussing the sleeping arrangements in the house, was, 'I know you only sleep with Daddy because you don't have a bed of your own!'

Anthea Turner.

(ANTHEA TURNER)

TV presenter

I have lived in this house my whole life but one day I found a hidden door. Inside was the most beautiful room I have ever seen. It's enormous! I have to clean it from top to toe every day and it constantly needs repainting and refurbishing. It takes up nearly all of my time and, although it infuriates me, I love it more than life itself. Now the door is open I can never close it. This is having children.

(ANNE DAVIES)

GMTV presenter

Three quick tips:

* Love and be nice to your children – they're the ones who'll choose your retirement home.

* Don't ever imagine that there is any substitute for giving your kids your time and attention.

* Never let a child wearing Superman pyjamas sleep on the top bunk!

(PETER MEADOWS)

Author of *The Parentalk Guide to Being a Dad*

Practise your BBC hair and make-up department skills because, if your children are anything like mine, they'll be wanting daily reincarnations as Barbie, the Spice Girls, Ariel the Little Mermaid and Sleeping Beauty, not to mention My Little Pony ...!

(LAURENCE LLEWELYN-BOWEN)

Designer and Presenter, *Changing Rooms*

OF COURSE I KNOW THE BOUNDARIES, DAD — SO CAN YOU GO AND TELL NEXT DOOR I'VE KICKED MY BALL THROUGH THEIR HEDGE?

The other day I asked the best parent I know the most important thing about raising children. She answered,

'Two things; first, that your children know that you love them unconditionally and, second, that they know where the boundaries are. Both these things bring security.'

Who is this wise lady? My wife Janet, the mother of my children!

(GARY STREETER MP)

Having children is a bit like writing songs. You do your very best to create something of beauty and meaning. You love them and pass on the little wisdom you might have, you send them off into the world and hope they will be loved by, and be of use to, others. If not careful you can offload on them too much and darken their souls for no worthy reason. They will often surprise you with insights into your own world that you never quite saw and, if you're lucky, they may even come back smiling to pay the odd bill. Above all, though you create and shape, love and hone, they don't belong to you, they pass through your hands on their way to creating their own melodies.

(MARTYN JOSEPH)

Singer/Songwriter

The hardest part of my job at the Millennium Dome is being apart from my 4-year-old daughter. She is a huge inspiration to me and, however hard my job is, a simple phone call from her telling me she loves me always reminds me there's far more to life than work (and golf!)

(PIERRE-YVES GERBEAU)

Chief Executive, New Millennium Experience Company

My son, now twelve, changed school when he was in Year 5. He had already done sex education in his previous school and therefore felt quite experienced and knowing about the subject.

On one day he said to me that the sex education lessons would be boring as he already knew all about 'the egg getting into the Oval'! (He'd been taken to the cricket ground the previous week and I think he'd got a bit mixed up!)

(ANNIE HULLEY)

Gwen Davies in *Coronation Street*

I spent many years standing in the hall at the foot of the stairs screaming, 'Turn that noise down!' while the latest in a run of peculiar young bands loudly entertained my kids via their recently released CDs.

Then came a period of silence while they attended university. The peace and tranquillity was heaven-sent at first, but funnily enough there came a period of longing. So much so that when they came home for a vacation I found myself standing in the hall screaming up the stairs, 'Turn that noise up!'

Little treasures!

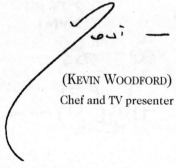

(KEVIN WOODFORD)
Chef and TV presenter

He never listened to a single word I said!

(ADA CHALKE)

Mother of Steve

Useful Addresses

ORGANISATIONS

Parentline Plus
520 Highgate Studios
53-76 Highgate Road
Kentish Town
London NW5 1TL
HELPLINE: 0808 800 2222
TEXTPHONE:0800 783 6783
FAX: 020 7284 5501
E-MAIL:
centraloffice@parentlineplus.
org.uk
WEBSITE:
www.parentlineplus.org.uk

*Provides freephone helpline
called Parentline and courses
for parents via the Parent
Network Service. Parentline
Plus also includes the National
Stepfamily Association. For all
information call the Parentline
freephone number on
0808 800 2222.*

Parentalk
PO Box 23142
London SE1 OZT
TEL: 0700 2000 500
FAX: 020 7450 9060
E-MAIL: info@parentalk.co.uk
WEBSITE: www.parentalk.co.uk

*Provides a range or resources
and services designed to
inspire and equip parents to
make the most of parenthood.*

**National Family and
Parenting Institute**
430 Highgate Studios
53-79 Highgate Road
London NW5 1TL
TEL: 020 7424 3460
FAX: 020 7485 3590
E-MAIL: info@nfpi.org
WEBSITE: www.nfpi.org

*An independent charity set up
to provide a strong national
focus on parenting and families
in the 21st century.*

93

Fathers Direct
Tamarisk House
37 The Tele Village
Crickhowell Powys NP8 1BP
TEL: 01873 810 515
WEBSITE: www.fathersdirect.com

Information resource for fathers.

**National Stepfamily
Association** now part of
Parentline Plus.
*For all information call the
Parentline freephone number
on 0808 800 2222.*

**National Council for One
Parent Families**
255 Kentish Town Road
London NW5 2LX
Lone Parent Line:
0800 018 5026
Maintenance & Money Line: 020
7428 5424
(Mon & Fri 10.30 am–1.30 pm
Wed 3 pm–6 pm)

*Information service for lone
parents.*

Dads & Lads
Dirk Uitterdijk
Andy Howie
YMCA England National Dads
& Lads project
Dee Bridge House
25–27 Lower Bridge Street
Chester CH1 1RS
TEL: 01244 403090
E-MAIL:
dirk@parenting.ymca.org.uk
ahowie@themail.co.uk

*Locally based projects run
jointly by YMCA and Care for
the Family for fathers and sons,
mentors and boys. They offer a
unique opportunity to get
together with other fathers and
sons for a game of football and
other activities. To find out
where your nearest Dads &
Lads project is based or to get
help starting a new one, please
contact Dirk Uitterdijk at the
above address.*

Gingerbread
16-17 Clerkenwell Close
London EC1R OAA
TEL: 020 7336 8183
FAX: 020 7336 8185
E-MAIL:
office@gingerbread.org.uk
WEBSITE:
www.gingerbread.org.uk

*Provides day-to-day support
and practical help for lone
parents.*

Kidscape
2 Grosvenor Gardens
London SW1W ODH
TEL: 020 7330 3300
FAX: 020 7330 7081
E-MAIL: info@kidscape.org.uk
WEBSITE: www.kidscape.org.uk

*Works to prevent the abuse of
children through education
programmes involving parents
and teachers, providing a
range of resources. Also runs a
bullying helpline.*

**Positive Parenting
Publications**
1st Floor
2A South Street
Gosport PO12 1ES
TEL: 01705 528787
FAX: 01705 501111
E-MAIL: info@parenting.org.uk
WEBSITE: www.parenting.org.uk

*Aims to prepare people for the
role of parenting by helping
parents, those about to become
parents and also those who
lead parenting groups.*

**Relate: National Marriage
Guidance**
National Headquarters
Herbert Gray College
Little Church Street
Rugby
Warwickshire CV21 3AP
TEL: 01788 573241
FAX: 01788 535007
E-MAIL:
enquiries@national.relate.org.uk
WEBSITE: www.relate.org.uk

NSPCC
NSPCC National Centre
42 Curtain Road
London EC2A 3NH
TEL: 020 7825 2500
FAX: 020 7825 2525
WEBSITE: www.nspcc.org.uk
HELPLINE NUMBER:
0800 800 500

*Aims to prevent child abuse
and neglect in all its forms and
give practical help to families
with children at risk.*

*The NSPCC also produces
leaflets with information and
advice on positive parenting –
020 7825 2500.*

Care for the Family
PO Box 488
Cardiff CF15 7YY
TEL: 029 2081 0800
FAX: 029 2081 4089
E-MAIL:
care.for.the.family@cff.org.uk
WEBSITE: www.care-for-the-
family.org.uk

*Providing support for families
through seminars, resources
and special projects.*

PARENTING COURSES

Parentalk Parenting Course
*A new parenting course
designed to give parents the
opportunity to share their
experiences, learn from each
other and discover some
principles of parenting.*

Parentalk
PO Box 23142
London SE1 OZT

For more information phone
0700 2000 500

**Positive Parenting
Publications**
*Publishes a range of low cost,
easy to read, common sense
resource materials which
provide help, information and
advice. Responsible for running
a range of parenting courses
across the UK. For more
information phone
01705 528787.*

Parent Network
*For more information call
Parentline Plus on
0808 800 2222.*